An Exchange Rate Target
Why we need one

An Exchange Rate Target
Why we need one

John Mills

Civitas: Institute for the Study of Civil Society
London

First Published April 2013

© Civitas 2013
55 Tufton Street
London SW1P 3QL

email: books@civitas.org.uk

All rights reserved

ISBN 978-1-906837

Independence: Civitas: Institute for the Study of Civil Society is a registered educational charity (No. 1085494) and a company limited by guarantee (No. 04023541). Civitas is financed from a variety of private sources to avoid over-reliance on any single or small group of donors.

All publications are independently refereed. All the Institute's publications seek to further its objective of promoting the advancement of learning. The views expressed are those of the authors, not of the Institute.

Typeset by Kevin Dodd
Printed in Great Britain by
Berforts Group Ltd
Stevenage SG1 2BH

Contents

	Page
Author	vi
Foreword	vii
Introduction	1
1. Standard of Living	4
2. Unemployment	7
3. Dependency	10
4. Debt	12
5. The Welfare State	15
6. Inequality	18
7. Britain's Place in the World	21
8. Remedies	24
Notes	31

Author

John Mills is an entrepreneur and economist. He graduated in Politics, Philosophy and Economics from Merton College, Oxford, in 1961. He is currently chairman of John Mills Limited, a highly successful import-export and distribution company.

He has been Secretary of the Labour Euro-Safeguards Campaign since 1975 and the Labour Economic Policy Group since 1985. He has also been a committee member of the Economic Research Council since 1997 and is now Vice-Chairman. He is also Chairman of The People's Pledge campaign for a referendum on Britain's EU membership.

He is the author of *Growth and Welfare: A New Policy for Britain* (Martin Robertson and Barnes and Noble 1972); *Monetarism or Prosperity?* (with Bryan Gould and Shaun Stewart Macmillan 1982); *Tackling Britain's False Economy* (Macmillan 1997); *Europe's Economic Dilemma* (Macmillan 1998); *America's Soluble Problems* (Macmillan 1999); *Managing the World Economy* (Palgrave Macmillan 2000); *A Critical History of Economics* (Palgrave Macmillan 2002 and Beijing Commercial Press 2006); and *Exchange Rate Alignments* (Palgrave Macmillan 2012).

He is also the author of a previous Civitas pamphlet, *A Price That Matters* (Civitas 2012).

Foreword

A number of countries have become alarmed that their exchange rate is too high, including Switzerland and Japan. Their corrective policies have been criticised by some economists for increasing the risk of a 'currency war'.* According to their abstract reasoning, a policy of 'competitive devaluations' may harm international trade, despite being ultimately futile for the simple reason that other countries retaliate, leaving relative prices unaltered.

But this kind of thinking attaches too little weight to the objective differences between nations. In particular, a nation with a long-standing trade deficit ought to be free to encourage its currency to fall in value, so that its export prices will be lower, thus giving it a fighting chance of achieving a trade balance. Indeed, economic theory assumes that, when the value of a nation's currency is allowed to float in a freely-adjusting market, it will tend to fall in value when there is a trade deficit for the obvious reason that demand for its currency has fallen.

As John Mills shows, the UK has had a significant trade deficit in goods for about 30 years and an overall current-account deficit for nearly as long. The value of the pound should fall. Demand for the pound has been kept artificially high because we have been selling off our businesses and high-end residential properties to overseas owners and selling government bonds to non-UK residents. This extra demand for

---

* http://www.telegraph.co.uk/finance/financialcrisis/9816996/Jens-Weidmann-warns-of-currency-war-risk.html

our currency has tipped the balance against our manufacturers, despite the massive and sustained improvements in productivity they have achieved in recent years.

If international trade is to be mutually beneficial, then it is vital that the market should be free to adjust the value of currencies according to trade flows. A nation that maintains a long-term surplus by artificially weakening its currency, as China does, is not treating trade as a mutually beneficial process of extending prosperity to all. It is treating trade as a struggle for supremacy – a kind of economic warfare.

Our long-standing trade deficit means that we are fully entitled to adopt policies that push down the value of the pound until we have a trade balance. The aim of policy should not be to promote a continuous surplus, but rather a trade balance. Only if nations accept that trade must be mutually beneficial, with no one country seeking a long-term surplus at the expense of others, can international trade fulfil its moral purpose of providing a framework for the discovery of the most efficient producers of goods and services that consumers want.

David G. Green

Introduction

The UK is still a good place to live compared with many other countries in the world, so a sense of proportion about our current travails is required. All the same, our economy and society evidently display a number of problems, all of which have become more conspicuous and serious over recent decades. Growth has all but disappeared as the economy dips in and out of recession. Unemployment is much higher than it was during the years following World War II. There is a significant minority of people who have been out of work for so long that they are now outside the traditional work ethic. The total liabilities of the government are getting closer to being unmanageably large. The welfare state is becoming more and more expensive to maintain while the government's ability to pay for it – and at the same time meet all its other obligations and liabilities – is increasingly uncertain. Our place both in the European Union and in the wider world is in doubt as our relative power and influence decline. There are now huge disparities not only in wealth and income but life chances generally, both between people at varying socio-economic levels and between different regions of the country. These are all serious problems, and they are all generally much more acute than they were only a few decades ago.

Do all these problems have a common cause? Is there an underlying reason why all these unwanted trends have materialised broadly at the same time? If so, is there anything that can be done to reverse them? Life is too complex for there ever to be one simple solution to complicated problems. Any major change in policy to ameliorate the underlying cause of our current difficulties would therefore undoubtedly require many complementary changes in strategy to be put in train at the same time. If, however, all the major problems detailed above have, at least in part, a common cause which the government might be able to tackle, then dealing with them could become much more manageable. Even if there is no magic wand which could be waved to solve all our problems, policy changes which could improve matters in some key respects relatively easily might be able to clear the ground for tackling other undesirable and more difficult to deal with features of our society and economy.

The thesis put forward in this pamphlet is that the key common feature to all the social and economic problems listed above lies with the way in which economic policies in the UK have been implemented over a long period, but particularly during the last four decades since the early 1970s. It is the way in which we have run our economy that is primarily responsible for the way all of them have materialised. We could have adopted different policies – and we could still do so – so the strains we are currently facing should not be as intractable as they might appear. If we continue as we are, however, it is all too likely that all the problems described above will get worse. There is, therefore, a lot at stake.

What has gone wrong with the economy? What is causing or facilitating the accumulation of so many pressing social and economic problems? Why does it seem to be so difficult to get our economy to grow and flourish compared with the successes achieved in other parts of the world? The key message in this pamphlet is that the fundamental reason for our economic problems is that we live in a country which has had steadily increasing difficulties in paying its way in the world. This manifests itself as a balance of payments deficit year after year. The last time we had a trade surplus in manufactured goods was 1982. We have not had a current account surplus including all its various components – with a possible exception in 1998[1] – since 1985[2]. For the last thirty years there has been a steepening trend towards the UK having a bigger and bigger deficit on our current account transactions with the rest of the world. This has a number of effects, the most important of which are:

- The loss of purchasing power in the economy as what we sell to the world is less than what we buy. This purchasing power has to be replaced elsewhere to stop demand falling to unacceptable levels

- The reluctance of policy makers to stimulate demand in the economy for fear of widening our trade deficit

- Reduced competitiveness as the resulting slow growth in economic output discourages investment

- The accumulation of debt as every pound of the current account deficit has to be matched exactly – as an accounting identity – by capital inflows or borrowing

The slow growth in output, the increasing debt needed to finance our continuing current account deficits and the resulting depressed state of the economy are the key factors linking all the economic and social problems with which this pamphlet is concerned.

1

The Standard of Living

Persistent weakness in our ability to pay our way in the world has had a hugely depressing effect on the capacity of the economy to grow. The UK experienced slower growth than most other developed countries for the first quarter century after 1945 but since then the growth rate of nearly all western countries has been on average about the same as that of the UK. The UK's performance for the 40 years from 1970 to 2010 has been a little worse than the world average but not by much. The really crucial measure here is GDP per head, which takes population growth into account. Over the 40 years between 1970 and 2010, the UK economy grew by 2.0%[3] per annum while the population increased by 11.7% i.e. 0.3% per annum, from 55.42m to 61.90m[4]. Living standards per head therefore grew over this period by 102% or 1.8% per annum. In the world as a whole the comparable figures were 3.6%[5] annual economic growth, 86.7% increase in population (from 3.70bn to 6.90bn)[6] and 117% growth in living standards, averaging 2.0% a year. In China, however, there was 8.4% economic growth per annum, 51.4% population growth (from 830m to 1,257m)[7] producing a 16.8 fold average increase in Chinese living standards over the 40 year period – averaging 7.5% a year.

The really crucial differences in growth rates over these four decades have therefore been between the fast growing Pacific Rim, where countries such as South Korea and Singapore have grown nearly as fast as China, and the rest of the world. It is in the latter group where the UK is located, comprising most of the Western world and also many slow growth developing countries. Apart from slow growth, many of these countries also share with the UK similar social and economic problems.

The figures for most of the Western world, including the UK, however, look much worse if widening distributions of income are taken into account. If the very substantial increases in income which have accrued to those who are best off are allowed for, the picture which is then left is one of median incomes growing much more slowly than mean incomes, while especially during the first decade of the twenty first century the poorest tenth of the UK's population actually experienced a fall in income of over 10%.[8]

The combination of slow growth and widening income differentials has thus been to leave a large section of the UK's population with very slowly growing living standards during recent decades, especially compared with what has happened in countries which have pursued much more successful economic policies. The prospects for the future, however, look even worse if there is little or no growth in the economy as a whole. Allowing then for both population growth and the potential for ever widening inequality caused by rising unemployment, it is likely that falling living standards are going to be the future for many millions of UK citizens. Between 2007 and 2011, UK average GDP per head fell by just under 8%.[9] Although most of the fall was in 2009, the economy's recovery since then has been anaemic.

It has dipped in and out of recession while the population continued to increase. This indicates that, on present trends, little optimism about any rise in most peoples' living standards is warranted.

For two hundred years or more, admittedly with occasional dips, people living in the UK have experienced significantly rising living standards. If the future is one with stagnant or falling living standards for a large proportion of the population, we are then moving into new and uncharted territory, especially if much of the rest of the world is steadily becoming more prosperous.

2

Unemployment

While unemployment was a major problem in the UK in the 1920s and 30s, by the end of World War II, there was almost no-one capable of working who was out of a job. This situation continued with minor fluctuations around an unemployment rate of about 3% until the early 1970s, when the world boom following the 1971 devaluation of the dollar ended, causing a sharp increase in the numbers who were out of work. For the next decade in the UK unemployment steadily increased, reaching a high point in 1984 of 12%. It then fell below 8% before climbing again at the beginning of the 1990s to almost 11%. It then dropped steadily to 5% until the financial crisis broke in 2007, since when it has climbed to almost 8%, with about 2.5m unemployed.[10]

Figures of 8% and 2.5m, however, only tell half the story. The reality is that the number of people in the UK of working age who are not working but who would do so if there were enough jobs available at reasonable wages is much higher than the headline unemployment rate implies. If the total includes all those who are not working because they are caught in benefit traps; or who have been signed off on long term sickness benefit by kindly doctors who could see no other way of providing them with adequate incomes; or who have been forced into early retirement; or who have given up hope of getting work, then the total is more than twice as high as the official figures – estimated at the beginning of 2012 by the TUC as being as high as 6.3m people altogether.[11]

The reason why so many people are without jobs has very little to do with the employability of the labour force. On the contrary it has everything to do with lack of sufficient purchasing power in the economy to provide everyone with work. Just as almost everyone of working age who was unemployed in the 1930s was in work by 1945, so exactly the same could be done again if only adequate demand was there. This is why training schemes and all the many other supply side remedies propounded to get the number of unemployed down in the absence of a sufficiently buoyant economy and adequate demand will never work. It is not lack of skills which is the fundamental problem, although obviously, other things being equal, the better skilled the workforce is, the better. It is lack of job opportunities.

Of course it is true that some people will always be more employable than others. It is also the case that, for a whole variety of reasons, the productivity of the employed labour force is slowly increasing, so that increased unemployment can take place even if the economy overall is gradually expanding. The crucial issue is whether it is growing fast enough – i.e. that total demand is keeping up with the aggregate capacity of the labour force to produce goods and services. It is because this has not happened over the last 40 years that unemployment has crept up to its current tragic levels.

This would be a disaster at any time, but it makes even less sense in current circumstances when demographic trends mean that the number of old age dependents is increasing. In 1975, for every 100 people of working age (15 to 64) in the economy, there were

22 dependents aged over 64. By 2011 there were 26. Nor is the working age population being replenished. In 1975, for every 100 people of working age there were 37 dependents under 15. In 2011 this had fallen to 26.[12] Unemployment on the scale currently experienced in the UK is not only a personal tragedy for everyone who would like to work but who is denied the opportunity to do so. It is also an economic millstone round our necks which we very urgently need to remove.

3

Dependency

As unemployment has increased, including among them the many hundreds of thousands of people who are not caught in the headline figures, so there has been a massive increase in the numbers of people who are no longer contributing to national income, at least within the formal economy caught by national statistics. No doubt the situation is not quite as official figures capture it because of the black economy, but there is no great evidence that the black economy is proportionately much larger now than it has ever been. Even if it was, all those working for cash in hand are still paying no tax and nearly all of them are drawing whatever benefits they would be entitled to if they were not moonlighting.

The very large majority of those who are unemployed do not, however, earn much which is not declared. Instead, they live a life which is largely supported by benefits paid by the state. Although the life style that is then possible is far from luxurious, for most people it is not unbearably low. If there are jobs available, for many people receiving UK benefits, the income offered is simply not high enough for it to be worth taking on all the obligations of being employed. It is not surprising, therefore, that there are millions of people who have dropped out of the labour force, see little merit in getting a job and whose work ethic has been sapped away. This is an extremely troubling social as well as economic development. It is not healthy for any society to have a large minority of its citizens who have dropped out of the labour force and all that being employed entails. Apart from anything else, it generates a large amount of resentment among those – often not on very high incomes themselves – who have to support the lifestyles of those who do not appear to have any interest in working. It also has corrosive effects in other ways. There is ample evidence that families where no one is working tend to lack positive role models and the parents therefore set their children off in life with major disadvantages. It is hardly surprising that children from families who have largely dropped out of the economy find much of their schooling an irrelevant experience to which they attach little value. More generally the lack of a self-help ethic, generated by months or years outside the employed labour force, can all too easily wash over into a view of the world in which individuals look to others to solve their problems rather than taking responsibility for their own well-being.

The inescapable conclusion is that a lack of sufficiently rewarded work opportunities – a direct result of the ineffective way in which our economy has been run – does not just have a heavy economic cost. It also has a large and deleterious impact on our social cohesion, while at the same time causing huge numbers of people to live much less productive and satisfying lives than ought to be possible.

4

Debt

Until comparatively recently, debt was not a major problem in the UK except as a result of wars, which certainly had a major impact on it. At the end of the Napoleonic Wars, government debt was over 250% of GDP. Just before World War I it was about 30%, rising to 175% by 1918. It was still about 125% at the start of World War II, by the end of which it stood at 230%. It then fell to no more than 25% by 1990, but since then it has risen to almost 70%.[13] It is still on a strong rising trend.

The difference between now and what happened in the past is that it is not wartime expenditures which have recently caused government debt to increase rapidly; it is the fact that the government in recent years has been unable to cover all its expenditures by the money it raises from taxation and charges. The reason that this has happened is undoubtedly due to the UK's overall poor economic performance. It has not occurred, however, as is sometimes alleged, because of profligate expenditure funded by inadequate income. There is a more fundamental and much more crucial reason why this trend has manifested itself.

The deficit on government expenditure is inextricably tied up with the current account deficit which has been such a constant feature of the UK's economy for the last two decades. Up to about 1985, the UK's current account was broadly speaking in balance, with an increasing deficit on manufactured goods and transfers abroad being offset by rising surpluses on services and net income. There was then a deterioration of the overall position towards the end of the 1980s, offset by an improvement after we left the Exchange Rate Mechanism in 1992, but by the end of the 1990s the position was deteriorating again.[14] During the 2000s the adverse trend markedly worsened. Between 2000 and 2010 the UK had a huge cumulative payments deficit of £287bn.[15]

This massive deficit sucked demand out of the economy as payments abroad exceeded those coming into the UK. Somehow this had to be replaced to avoid the effect on the economy being highly deflationary. There were three possible ways this could be done. One was for the corporate sector to invest more than its retained profits. The second was for consumers to spend more than their net incomes, with the balance being borrowed. The third was for the government to run a deficit. Up to 2007/08, there was sufficient buoyancy in the financial behaviour of the corporate world and among consumers to come fairly close to offsetting the deflationary effect of the foreign payments deficit. Once the financial crisis began, however, both business and financial confidence fell dramatically, leaving the government running a massive deficit as the only way of stopping the economy collapsing. This is why in 2009, the government net deficit rose to almost 10% of GDP, with the government borrowing one in five of every pound it spent.[16] This was essential as otherwise the UK economy would have experienced an even more severe depression than the one from which it was suffering already. In these circumstances it is hardly surprising that the increase in government debt between 2000 and 2010 – at a total of £471bn – came reasonably close to mirroring the total current account deficit over these years, which came to just under £300bn.

Two key lessons emerge from these considerations. The first is that as long as we have a deficit on our current account, and neither business nor consumers are able and willing to fill the deficiency in demand thus created, the government will have to do so, to avoid a massive shortage of purchasing power in the economy. There is no way, therefore, that the government is going to be able to get rid of its deficit unless the balance of payments position improves. The second is that, if present trends continue, the government's total debt is going to get out of control. It is only manageable at the moment because interest rates are low and the total sum is still no more than 70% of GDP. However, if the government's debt keeps rising much faster than the economy is growing – an all too likely scenario on current trends – the position will become unsustainable, particularly if the state's other commitments, such as public sector pensions, are taken into consideration. There is thus a very pressing need for the UK to put its current account into a much better position than it is at the moment.

5

The Welfare State

The problems faced by our over-stretched welfare state are not all the result of the UK's slow growth over the last few decades – although some are – but it is certainly arguable that implementation of the reforms which are clearly necessary is much more difficult against a background of austerity and falling resources than it would be were money more widely available.

The problem with the welfare state is that it has grown like topsy and, as a result, it has lost much of its rationality. There is certainly a very strong case for providing a large number of services on a communal basis, even if there are debatable borderline cases. Apart from the maintenance of law and order and the defence of the realm, which have always been regarded as being the responsibilities of the state, no one wants every road to be a toll road and few people think that the state has no role to play in health or education. There is also a strong welfare case for a reasonable amount of redistribution of income through the tax and benefit system, to even up at least in part the outcome of life's lottery, both between social classes and between different age groups. All of these objectives could comfortably be fulfilled with government expenditure taking up no more than perhaps 35% – maybe 40% at maximum – of national income. Government expenditure in the UK is, however, currently much more than this. In 2011 it came to 48%.[17]

The reason why it is so high is not because expenditure on communally provided services is particularly high or that public expenditure is especially redistributive. In fact, there is a fair amount of redistribution between roughly the top 5% of income earners and the bottom 20%. The trouble is that for all the remainder of the 75% of the population, public expenditure on a very wide variety of cash payments – from pensions to child benefit, from winter fuel payments to free bus fares – involves broadly the same people paying taxes to finance the benefits as those who receive them. The result is that the total amount of taxation almost everyone has to pay gets higher than most people think is reasonable. Not only does income tax start being paid at levels well below the average level, but also many indirect taxes, such as VAT, impact on poorer people more harshly than on those who are richer. At the same time, those with high incomes resent paying high income taxes to a point at which – rightly or wrongly – tax avoidance or evasion becomes much more tempting and financially rewarding than it would be if taxes were lower. There are two main problems about rationalising this structure. One is that it is very hard to do so without there being some immediate losers from any changes to be made, and they can be relied upon to complain much more loudly than the muted thanks heard from those who gain. The second is that lost benefits are much more visible than the reduced amount of taxation which would be required to finance them.

This is undoubtedly a very difficult area with no easy political solutions to hand with the economic prospects we are facing at the moment. There is, however, little doubt that it would be much easier to rationalise the way the welfare state operates if the economy was performing better, for two main reasons. One is that a significant proportion of the benefit payments which are made at present – and the tax foregone which might otherwise have been collected – are the direct result of the very high levels of unemployment we have. If almost everyone was in work and paying taxes instead of collecting benefits and certainly paying no income tax, this in itself would reduce the government's share of GDP by perhaps 5%. Second, if the economy was growing and total cash benefits were held roughly constant while GDP got larger, the proportion of GDP going through the government's hands would fall.

6

Inequality

There has always been a large gap between the income and wealth of those who are most and least well off in socio-economic terms, but inequality in the UK has got much greater since the 1970s. For those who are statistically minded, the UK's Gini co-efficient, which was 26 in 1979, is now 40, having steadily increased over all of the last three decades. As inequality slowly became greater, four fifths of the total increase in incomes over the decade between 2000 and 2010 went to those with above average incomes and two fifths went to those in the richest tenth. The income of the richest tenth is now more than the income of all those on below average income combined.[18]

The period between 1945 and 1970 saw much less inequality in the UK than ever before in its history. Some of this was due to government policies on redistribution of income and the much larger civilian role the state took on following the election of the Labour government in 1945. Much of the reduction in equality, however, stemmed from other factors, particularly the very full employment there was over this period. Another important contributor was the reasonable balance in prosperity between different regions of the country, for which the wide and fairly even dispersion of manufacturing industry over most of the country was responsible.

From the 1970s onwards, however, these vital props for keeping inequality at bay were removed. For the last four decades, unemployment – especially if those not included in the headline figures are included – has been on a remorseless upward trend. At the same time the UK has steadily deindustrialised, with fewer and fewer of the country's labour force employed in manufacturing. As late as 1980 28.3% of the UK's labour force worked in manufacturing industry.[19] By 2011, that percentage had fallen to 8.8% and by the third quarter of 2012 it was down to 8.3%.[20] As well-paid blue collar jobs have disappeared with the demise of manufacturing, employment in services has become even more dominant. In 1980, 61.2% of the working population were employed in the service sector. By 2011 that proportion had risen to 81.1%. Within this sector, there were much wider disparities in remuneration than generally applied in manufacturing. In 2012, mean gross value added (GVA) was £240 a week in 'Accommodation and Food' whereas it was £802 in 'Finance and Insurance'.[21] At one end of the spectrum are bankers and others in the City earning sums per annum beyond the dreams of avarice for most of the population while at the other end there are huge numbers of people working unconscionably long hours on no more than the minimum wage. This is not the best way to build a society which is at ease with itself, let alone one which is providing all its citizens with the best opportunities for leading fulfilling and rewarding lives.

There is also a huge regional as well as socio-economic dimension to inequality in the UK. During the height of the Industrial Revolution, standards of living were higher in the North of Britain than they were in the South, but this has now all changed. Recent figures show a staggering difference in the annual average GVA per worker in Greater London (£35,638) compared with the poorest region, the North East, where the comparable figure was £15,842.[22] Average gross weekly earnings may provide a better guide to actual living standards and in the second quarter of 2012 these were £719 in London and £462 in the North East.[23] Of course London is a much more expensive place to live than Newcastle, so the differences in living standards are not as stark as these comparisons might suggest. Even so, they are still very wide and there is little doubt why these enormous gaps have opened up. It is the collapse of so much manufacturing industry in the regions combined with the dominance of financial services in London which is very largely responsible.

7

Britain's Place in the World

Within the memory of many people alive today, Britain was at least partly responsible for the governance of a quarter of the world's land mass. Now we are a middling power with our influence steadily declining. During the nineteenth century, we were the workshop of the world. Now our shops are full of imported goods. In 1950, the UK was responsible for a quarter of all world exports. In 2011, we produced 2.7% of them.[24] During most of the nineteenth century, living standards in the UK were as high as anywhere in the world. In 2011, by most financial rankings (either nominal or GDP per head) we came in at 22nd.[25] On the rather more subjective but significant Human Development Index, we ranked 26th.[26]

In some respects, however, we still do well. In January 2013 Britain topped Monocle magazine's "soft power" ranking of world nations for the first time, ousting the USA from its previous leadership. "Soft power" assesses each country's influence in terms of politics, diplomacy, business, culture, sport and education rather than financial might and brute force. The success of the London Olympics, the popularity of the latest James Bond film and the global reach of UK media productions counted heavily in our favour. The education firm Pearson judged the UK to be 6th in the world in its overall education international league table.[27] Judged by most standards, Britain is still a much better place to live than many other countries, especially for the well off. Nevertheless the slide in the UK's rankings in other respects is not good for the national psyche.

It is clear that the much lower rankings we now achieve are very largely a reflection of the extent to which the UK has slid down the economic league table. The reason for the dominant position we held in many respects in the nineteenth century was because at that time we were more successful than other countries economically. Our GDP per head and hence our living standard were higher than elsewhere and this is what gave us the powerful military, diplomatic and commercial leverage which we had in that epoch. Now that we no longer have these advantages, our position in the world is much less significant.

Perhaps this does not matter that much, especially if in "soft power" terms we are doing well; although it is difficult to believe that most people don't care that we are steadily slipping down global economic league tables and thus becoming less and less important in world terms. In the longer term, however, there is at least one really crucial way in which it may count a great deal, depending on how much value is attached to liberal democracy as the way of ordering human affairs. The fact that authoritarian societies are often outperforming liberal democracies economically may have a profound effect on the way the world is governed. It was not so long ago that Francis Fukuyama published his book *The End of History and the Last Man* (1992), predicting that liberal democracy was the inevitable end state to which all jurisdictions would eventually turn. Twenty years on it is hard to be so confident. If most liberal democracies seem to be mired in economic and financial difficulties, with social problems which seem to be beyond rational solution, and with waning military and diplomatic power, the world may turn to more autocratic methods of ordering society which most people in the West would certainly not welcome.

8

Remedies

If all the economic and social problems described above have a common cause, which is the relatively poor economic performance exhibited by the British economy over a long period but particularly over the last 40 years, are there policies available which would have a reasonable chance of providing a better future than what we are currently promised? Is there really no alternative to the austerity, continuing high unemployment, stagnating incomes, increasing debt, overstretched welfare state, rising inequality and declining national influence which otherwise looks likely to be our lot for as far ahead as anyone can see? This pamphlet argues that there are realistic alternative policies to those being pursued at present, and that we very urgently need to adopt them.

The starting point is to realise that the root problem with the UK economy – shared by much of the Western world – is that we cannot pay our way in the world. We have a huge current account deficit every year – estimated in the 2012 Autumn Statement to be running currently at 4% of GDP, or about £65bn per annum.[28] As we have seen, this deficit sucks demand out of the economy which, in the absence of sufficient business confidence to invest, then has to be replaced by expenditure financed by either excessive consumer or government borrowing. It is our weak balance of payments position which has caused both consumer and particularly government borrowing to rise to increasingly unsustainable levels, because all current deficits have to be matched pound for pound by capital receipts – mostly rising debt.

The major reason why we have such a large current account deficit every year is that we have a huge trade deficit, especially for manufactured goods. Nearly two thirds of our exports and three quarters of our imports are goods rather than services.[29] The only way, therefore, for us to be able to avoid trade deficits is for us to sell more manufactured goods to the rest of the world. Services will never be able to fill the gap. The reason why we have an annual £100bn deficit on manufactured goods is that it costs much more to manufacture almost anything here than in many other parts of the world, especially the Far East. Huge swathes of the world's manufacturing capacity have therefore migrated from the UK and other western countries to the Pacific Rim.

The reason why manufacturing in the UK is so expensive compared to elsewhere is that the cost base in the UK is so high. The cost base encompasses all locally incurred charges. Typically, including wages and salaries, these amount to about 60% of total manufacturing costs. There is no reason why the cost base in the UK should be charged out at a higher rate than is done by other countries. This is entirely an exchange rate issue. The very high UK charge out rate is the direct result of hugely expensive and mistaken policies pursued here for many decades, which have kept the exchange rate much too strong. These were greatly exacerbated by the monetarist policies pursued from the 1970s onwards to combat inflation, which forced up the exchange rate by over 60% between 1977 and 1982. With some fluctuations, it has stayed at this far too high level ever since.

The only policy which will remedy these problems is to get the UK cost base down to a level which will make it possible for us to re-establish enough manufacturing capacity to enable us to compete in the world. To do this, some fairly simple calculations show that we need to get the pound down by about a third from where it is now – to around $1.05 or €0.80. These calculations are based on the wealth of statistics which are available on the propensity of both exports and imports to respond to changes in the exchange rate, the most recent being one published by the IMF in 2010.[30] These show beyond any reasonable doubt that the UK balance of payments would be in much better shape following a devaluation although it would take two or three years for the full benefit to come through, because export volumes take longer to respond to price changes than imports. A depreciation of about 33% is of the same order of magnitude as the devaluation which took place in 1931 when the UK left the Gold Standard, precipitating high growth between 1932 and 1937 – cumulatively over 4% per annum. All the available statistical data suggest that a similar sized depreciation now would therefore be sufficient both to increase the growth rate to 3%–4% per annum and to bring unemployment down over a period of time to perhaps 3%. If these objectives could be achieved, all the other problems described in this pamphlet would clearly then become much easier to tackle.

Why don't we do it? There are two main reasons why this is not currently on many people's policy agenda. One is fear that such a policy would not work. The other is that for almost all the last century and a half British exchange rate policy has been broadly orientated to keeping sterling as strong as possible and it would be a wrenching change to move to a different strategy. A big part of the reason why this change is difficult is a series of misapprehensions, the key ones being:

- It is widely believed that devaluation produces more inflation than would have occurred anyway. This simply is not true, as can easily be seen by looking at historical statistics. It did not happen, for example, when we left the Exchange Rate Mechanism in 1992. Inflation fell from 5.9% in 1991 to 3.7% in 1992 and to 1.6% in 1993 before stabilising for the next few years at about 3%.[31]

- It is not true that devaluation reduces living standards. If the growth rate increases, the average standard of living must go up. Again 1992 provides a typical example. Allowing for population growth, GDP per head rose 0.3% in 1990, fell 2.0% in 1991 and was static in 1992 before growing by 2.0% in 1993 and 4.0% in 1994. It seems counter-intuitive that reducing the value of the pound on the foreign exchanges would make everyone in the UK better off on average – but this is what would happen.

- It is also not true that governments cannot change the exchange rate if they want to do so. There are many examples showing that this can be done. The UK government pursued policies which raised it by over 60% between 1977 and 1982. Implementing opposite policies would have the reverse effects. The most conspicuously successful example of this was the 1985 Plaza Accord between the USA and Japan, which reduced the value of the then grossly overvalued dollar by 46% against the Japanese Yen.[32]

- It is very unlikely that other countries either would or could retaliate against us. The dollar is a reserve currency. The Eurozone has many other preoccupations at present. Our share of world trade is now so small that countries such as China would hardly notice the change – as indeed happened between 2007 and 2009, during which the pound dropped from an annual average of $2.00 in 2007 to a low of $1.56 in 2009, before stabilising at $1.60 in 2011.[33]

- It is not true that we have tried devaluation before and found that it does not work. All the major devaluations which have taken place in the past – 1931, 1949, 1967, 1992 and 2007/09 – were forced upon us by balance of payments crises and in nearly all cases did no more than reduce the pound from being grossly over-valued to being a little less so. The exception was the 1931 devaluation which produced a spurt of growth – at 4.4% cumulatively per annum between 1933 and 1937 – which was the fastest rate of growth the UK economy has ever achieved over a four year period. Unfortunately, towards the end of the 1930s the pound rose strongly against other currencies as the Gold Block countries and the USA devalued. Sterling then became as over-valued as it had been before[34] and economic growth declined despite rearmament[35].

It is true, however, that if the pound went down by a third, imports and foreign holidays would be more expensive. It is also true that all the politicians, civil servants, commentators and academics who have supported policies to keep inflation down as top priority would have to change their mind-set to understanding that getting the exchange rate right is a much more important goal. Changing accepted orthodoxy is likely to be much the biggest obstacle to getting policies for the UK back on track despite the fact that neither the Coalition nor Labour policies for reducing the government deficit will work. Cutting government expenditure will deflate the economy but the consequent falling tax revenue and the mounting cost of unemployment will make the public expenditure gap impossible to close. Reflating the economy with the exchange rate where it is at the moment would be equally self-defeating. It would destabilise the markets and put our credit rating at risk, thus almost certainly raising interest rates and borrowing costs. The reality is that there are no solutions to our current economic problems other than increasing our competitiveness and paying our way in the world.

These solutions will remain out of reach without a competitive devaluation of sterling. Although of course many complementary supply side policies will be needed to take advantage of the opportunities which a much more competitive environment will create. It is all these steps taken together which will allow us to use our labour force to the full, gain a sufficient share of world trade and put us back on the path to prosperity.

Of course, persuading everyone to take a very different view on something as central as economic policy is not easy. The benefits of doing so, however, would be huge. If we really want to successfully tackle many of the economic and social problems which dog our economy at present, there is no alternative.

Notes

1. IMF figures show a deficit in 1998 but ONS figures show a very small surplus.
2. Pages 982 and 983 in *International Financial Statistics Yearbook 2000*. Washington DC: IMF.
3. Pages 164 and 165 in *International Financial Statistics Yearbook 2000* and page 76 in the same publication for 2011.
4. Ibid page 984 in the 2000 publication and 745 in the one for 2011.
5. Ibid pages 164 and 165 in the 2000 publication and page 76 in the one for 2011.
6. World Bank Databank Website:
   http://databank.worldbank.org/data/home.aspx
7. Page 346 in *International Financial Statistics Yearbook 2000* and page 232 in 2010 edition.
8. Changes in Real Income table on website www.poverty.org.uk:
   http://www.poverty.org.uk/09/index.shtml?2
9. Pages 76 and 753 in *International Financial Statistics Yearbook 2012*.
10. UK Unemployment Rate table in www.tradingeconomics.com:
    http://www.tradingeconomics.com/united-kingdom/unemployment-rate.
11. TUC press release, '"Total" Unemployed is 6.3 million', 13th January 2012:
    http://www.tuc.org.uk/economy/tuc-20616-f0.cfm
12. Age Dependency Ratio table in www.tradingeconomics.com:
    http://www.tradingeconomics.com/united-kingdom/age-dependency-ratio-percent-of-working-age-population-wb-data.html
13. Guardian/ONS national debt data:
    http://www.guardian.co.uk/news/datablog/2010/oct/18/deficit-debt-government-borrowing-data
14. Pages 982 and 983 in *International Financial Statistics Yearbook 2000*.
15. ONS Pink Book 2012, Table 1.1.
16. Pages 752 and 753 in *International Financial Statistics Yearbook 2012*.
17. Ibid pages 752 and 753.
18. Department of Work and Pensions figures quoted on website www.poverty.org.uk:
    http://www.poverty.org.uk/09/index.shtml?2
19. Table 7 in International Labour Comparisons, website www.bls.gov: http://www.bls.gov/fls/flscomparelf/tables.htm#table07_emsec

20. ONS ad hoc data and analysis, 'Productivity Jobs and hours, Market sector workers and hours', file reference 000950: http://www.ons.gov.uk/ons/about-ons/what-we-do/publication-scheme/published-ad-hoc-data/economy/january-2013/index.html
21. ONS unpublished table on Gross Value Added by Industrial Classification.
22. Page 2 in ONS Regional Gross Value Added (Income Approach) December 2012: http://www.ons.gov.uk/ons/rel/regional-accounts/regional-gross-value-added — income-approach-/december-2012/stb-regional-gva-2011.html
23. January 2013 ONS Labour Market Statistics, Table 'EARN 05': http://www.ons.gov.uk/ons/publications/re-reference-tables.html?edition=tcm%3A77-222531
24. Page 67 in *International Financial Statistics Yearbook 2012*.
25. For example, see World Bank website: http://data.worldbank.org/indicator/NY.GDP.PCAP.CD
26. 2011 United Nations Human Development Index: http://hdr.undp.org/en/media/HDR_2011_EN_Table1.pdf
27. Referenced in BBC website report 27th November 2012: http://www.bbc.co.uk/news/education-20498356
28. Page 86 in HM Treasury, *Autumn Statement 2012*: http://cdn.hm-treasury.gov.uk/autumn_statement_2012_complete.pdf
29. ONS Statistical Bulletin, Balance of Payments 3rd Quarter 2012 Table B: http://www.ons.gov.uk/ons/publications/re-reference-tables.html?edition=tcm%3A77-286024
30. *A Method for Calculating Export Supply and Import Demand Elasticities.* Working Paper WP/10/180. Washington DC: IMF, 2010: http://www.imf.org/external/pubs/ft/wp/2010/wp10180.pdf
31. Table on Historical UK Inflation in website www.safalra.com: http://safalra.com/other/historical-uk-inflation-price-conversion/
32. 'Did the Plaza Accord Cause Japan's Lost Decades?' IMF 2011: http://www.imf.org/external/pubs/ft/weo/2011/01/c1/box1_4.pdf
33. Pacific Exchange Rate Service: http://fx.sauder.ubc.ca/etc/GBPpages.pdf
34. *1948 Economic Commission for Europe Report*.
35. Table UK.1 in *Economic Statistics 1900-1983* by Thelma Liesner, London: The Economist, 1985.